THE WORLD OF ART

WATER

through the eyes of artists

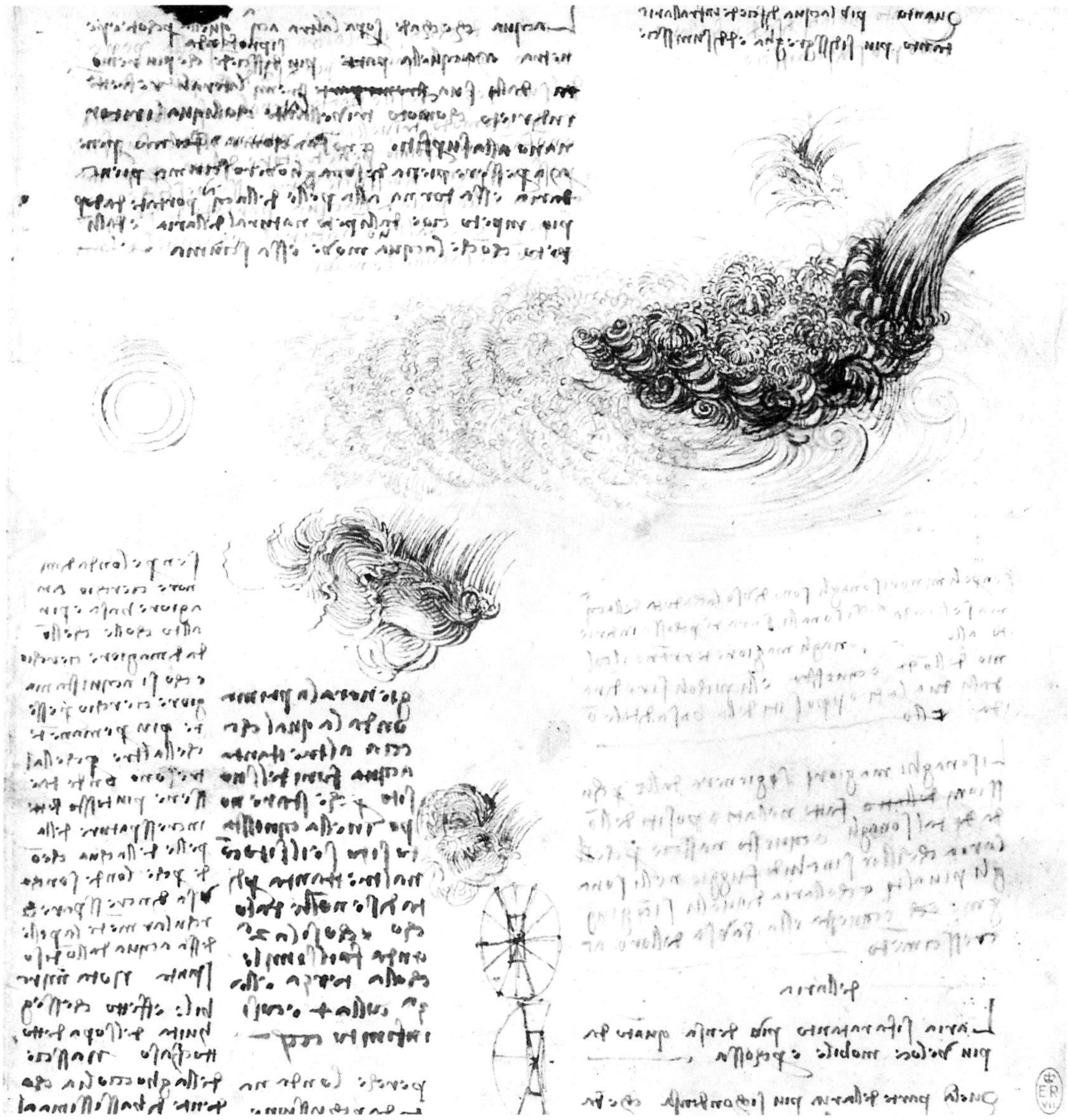

Windsor Castle, Royal Library © Her Majesty The Queen

Wendy and Jack Richardson

M
MACMILLAN

First published 1990

Published by Macmillan Children's Books
A division of MACMILLAN PUBLISHERS LTD.
Houndmills, Basingstoke, Hampshire RG21 2XS and London

Companies and representatives throughout the world

Picture research by Faith Perkins

Printed in Hong Kong

British Library Cataloguing in Publication Data

Richardson, Wendy
Water
1. Paintings Special Subjects, Water
I. Title II. Richardson, Jack III. Series
758'.95537

ISBN 0-333-47566-6

Photographic acknowledgements
The authors and publishers wish to acknowledge with thanks the following photographic sources:

Drawings and Notes on Water – Windsor Castle, Royal Library © Her Majesty The Queen piii
Kitty Kielland – Nasjonalgalleriet, Oslo pvi
Lorrain – (The Mary Evans Picture Library) p8
The Embarkation of the Queen of Sheba – The National Gallery, London p9
Turner – The National Portrait Gallery, London p10
The Shipwreck – The Tate Gallery p11
Whistler – The Detroit Institute of Arts, Bequest of Henry Glover Stevens in memory of Ellen P. Stevens and Mary M. Stevens p12
The Blue Wave – Hill-stead Museum, Connecticut p13
Georgia O'Keeffe – Metropolitan Museum of Art, New York p14
Wave, Night – Addison Gallery of American Art, Phillips Academy, Andover, Massachusetts p15
Mt Fuji Across the Water – Reproduced by courtesy of the Trustees of the British Museum p17
John Houston – John Houston p18
Sunset over the Sea – Watercolour – © John Houston p19
Sunset over the Sea – Tapestry – © John Houston – The Edinburgh Tapestry Co. Ltd p19
Kitty Kielland – Nasjonalgalleriet, Oslo p20
Sommernatt – Nasjonalgalleriet, Oslo p21
Arthur Boyd – (Photograph Jorge Lewinski) p22
Jinker on a Sandbank – Fischer Fine Art p23
Kokoschka – Museum of Modern Art, New York © COSMOPRESS, Geneva/DACS London 1988 (The Bridgeman Art Library) p24
Lac d'Annecy – The Phillips Collection, Washington © COSMOPRESS, Geneva/DACS London 1988 p25
Fur Traders Descending the Missouri – The Metropolitan Museum of Art, New York, Morris K. Jessup Fund, 1933 p27
Monet – The Tate Gallery, London © DACS 1988 p28
Morning on the Seine near Giverny – The Metropolitan Museum of Art, New York, Bequest of Julian W Emmons, 1956 © DACS 1988 p29
Monet – The Tate Gallery, London © DACS 1988 p30
The Banks of the Seine near Vétheuil – National Gallery of Art, Washington, Chester Dale Collection © DACS 1988 p31
Seurat – Philadelphia Institute of Art (Visual Arts Library) p32
Bridge at Courbevoie – Courtauld Institute Galleries, London – The Bridgeman Art Library p33
The River – National Gallery of Art, Washington, Chester Dale Collection © DACS 1988 p35
Pollock – (Visual Arts Library) p36
The Deep – Musée D'Art Moderne, Paris © ARS 1988 (Photograph Art Resource) p37
Goyulan Bark No.3 – © Australian Institute of Aboriginal Studies p39
Hockney – (Camera Press) p40
A Diver 1978 – © David Hockney p41
Patrick Procktor – Photograph Duncan Baxter (Camera Press) p42
Leaping Cataract, Victoria Falls – © Patrick Procktor. The Redfern Gallery, London p43
Downpour at Shona – Hiraki Ukiyo-e Foundation. Riccar Art Museum, Tokyo p45
Van Gogh – The Metropolitan Museum of Art, New York, Gift of Miss Adelaide Milton de Groot, 1967 p46
Rain at Aviers – National Museum of Wales, Cardiff p47

Cover painting:
Mt Fuji Across the Water – Reproduced by courtesy of the Trustees of the British Museum

The publishers have made every effort to trace the copyright holders, but if they have inadvertently overlooked any, they will be pleased to make the necessary arrangements at the first opportunity.

Introduction

This is a book of pictures about water. Some of the paintings are old, and some have been made quite recently. Some are drawings, some are prints, some are paintings and one is a tapestry. They come from all over the world.

All the pictures look very different, but they have one thing in common. They were painted by people who had an idea about water and thought that the best way to share it was through a picture. So this is a book for you to look at.

Water fascinates us all. Artists have painted the deep sea and the ocean edge, rivers and lakes, freezing cold water and swimming pool water, pouring rain and cascading waterfalls. They have painted water calm and angry, giving pleasure and causing fear. Take a careful look at the pictures to see if you can find out what these painters hoped to tell us through their work.

Contents

		PAGE
Seaport: The Embarkation of the Queen of Sheba	*Claude*	8
The Shipwreck	*Turner*	10
The Blue Wave: Biarritz	*Whistler*	12
Wave, Night	*O'Keeffe*	14
Fuji seen through the Waves off Kanagawa	*Hokusai*	16
Sunset over the Sea	*Houston*	18
Summer Night	*Kielland*	20
Jinker on a Sandbank	*Boyd*	22
Lac d'Annecy II	*Kokoschka*	24
Fur Traders descending the Missouri	*Bingham*	26
Early Morning on the Seine	*Monet*	28
The Banks of the Seine near Vétheuil	*Monet*	30
The Bridge at Courbevoie	*Seurat*	32
The River	*Vlaminck*	34
The Deep	*Pollock*	36
Untitled	*Mundrugmundrug*	38
A Diver (Paper Pool No. 17)	*Hockney*	40
Leaping Cataract, Victoria Falls	*Procktor*	42
Downpour at Shono	*Hiroshige*	44
Landscape in the Rain	*Van Gogh*	46
Some ideas		48

Seaport: The Embarkation of the Queen of Sheba

Oil on canvas 148.6 × 193.7cm

Claude Gellee (Le Lorrain)

LIVED:
1600-1682

NATIONALITY:
French

TYPE OF WORK:
landscape paintings, drawings, etchings

Claude Gellee, who is usually referred to by his first name only, was a Frenchman who fell in love with the Italian countryside as a young man. He spent most of his life in Italy, painting large, picturesque scenes set in the plains and hills he loved. Claude usually chose a story from the Bible or from mythology as the excuse for a picture. His work has a dreamlike quality. It is like a vision of a past which never existed. Claude was really more interested in the setting of his pictures than the story. This picture is typical. You have to look hard to find the Queen of Sheba! She is tiny against the elegant buildings, the glowing aquamarine sea and the magical sky.

Careful composition

The picture is carefully composed so that the beautiful buildings, with their classical proportions, form a frame. The lines of the buildings also lead the eye into the picture. It is this use of architectural perspective which gives the scene depth. If you place a ruler along any of the edges of stone which appear to go back into the picture you will see that they all meet in one place. These lines converge at the boat in front of the round tower. This method of suggesting depth was invented by Italian painters in the fifteenth century. It needed careful measurement to get it exactly right. The main purpose of the architecture in the picture is to help in this way. It also gives a grandeur to the setting. It does not look much like a real seaport, does it?

Colour is another means of giving a picture depth. Both the sea and the sky fade from dark to light tones towards the horizon. Objects in the picture also seem to be smaller the more distant they become from us.

The search for the picturesque

This picture has, at first, the look of a real place. Yet if you study it, you will begin to see all sorts of exaggerations. Is the water ever that deep green at the edge? Would you see people arranged in quite such artistic, colourful groups at a busy seaport?

The National Gallery, London

The Shipwreck

Oil on canvas 171.5 × 249.9cm

Joseph Mallord William Turner

LIVED:
1775-1851

NATIONALITY:
British

TYPE OF WORK:
landscape paintings drawings,
engravings

The National Portrait Gallery, London

Joseph Turner's talent was recognized early in his life. He became a student at the Royal Academy School when he was only fourteen years old, and exhibited his first watercolour at the Academy a year later. When he was thirty-two years old he became Professor of Perspective at the Academy.

Travelling with a notebook

In 1792 Turner began a series of journeys that was to last his lifetime. He travelled first in Britain, and then throughout Europe making sketches and visual 'notes' of landscapes which interested him. Turner looked for the picturesque and the beautiful in nature. Sometimes he sold his drawings to engravers, and sometimes he reworked them himself in watercolour at a later date.

Influence from Europe

Turner's travels in France and Italy introduced him to the work of many painters. Turner said that it was the French painter Claude, whose work he admired most (see page 8). Early in the 1800s the style of Turner's work changed. His paintings took on a strong dramatic and romantic quality and he payed particular attention to the quality of light and the atmosphere in his pictures.

Movement and light

It is almost possible to feel seasick just from looking at this picture! The angles of the boats and the reaching arms of the boatman, the height of the boat on the right above the poor creatures caught in the trough of a wave in the centre all add to the drama. The monstrous swell itself, inky brown under a turbulent sky lashes itself to a murky and terrible cream. There is no end to it. The sea and sky merge in a crashing horizon.

A peculiar yellow light heightens the drama. It picks up the sails and the oddments of white clothing making the scene glitter in an unearthly way. In other works Turner paints gentle veils of hazy sunlight. Nothing is gentle here. This is a nightmare.

The Blue Wave: Biarritz

Oil on canvas 62.2 × 87.6 cm

James McNeill Whistler

LIVED:
1834-1903

NATIONALITY:
American

TYPE OF WORK:
portrait and landscape painting
lithography

Detail from Arrangement in Gray: Portrait of the Painter
© The Detroit Institute of Arts, Bequest of Henry Glover Stevens in memory of
Ellen P. Stevens and Mary M. Stevens

Though born in America, James McNeill Whistler spent most of his life in Europe. He lived in Russia as a child, and in Paris and London as an adult.

Revolutionary art

Whistler was a leader in the discussions about the arts and aesthetics which were taking place at the time. He had very definite ideas on art which he put into action in his own work. The general public and even the art critics found his paintings difficult to understand. They did not tell a story and they had no symbolism in them. They were not 'about anything'. Whistler became very cross when people tried to explain one of his paintings. It was a picture of a girl in a white dress against a white background, called simply, *The White Girl*. Some people said it was an illustration of a popular novel by Wilkie Collins, called *The Woman in White*. One critic said it was about a bride and her lost childhood which was symbolised by her white dress. Whistler could not make them understand that it was just a painting for looking at!

One famous critic called him a fraud who was 'flinging a pot of paint in the face of the public'. Whistler firmly believed that art was about art, not about emotions like patriotism, pity or love. Whistler expected people to respond to what they could *see* when they looked at his pictures. The paintings were about patterns and shapes and the subtle texture made by light and shade and colour, and nothing more. He began to give his paintings the sort of names that music had, for example *Nocturne in Blue and Silver: Chelsea* to try to explain that his work was to be looked at, just as music was to be listened to.

A harsh critic

Whistler was harshly self-critical, and while he complained of other critics, he was fierce in assessing his own work. He would often scrape off a whole picture, and he sometimes destroyed canvases which did not come up to his exacting standards. It is difficult for us to see today what seemed so strange about his work, as we have now learned to accept his ideas. Far stranger things have been done with paint since Whistler painted!

Hill-stead Museum, Connecticut

Wave, Night

Oil on canvas 75.9 × 91.5 cm

Georgia O'Keeffe

LIVED:
1887-1986

NATIONALITY:
American

TYPE OF WORK:
oil paintings, drawings

Metropolitan Museum of Art, New York

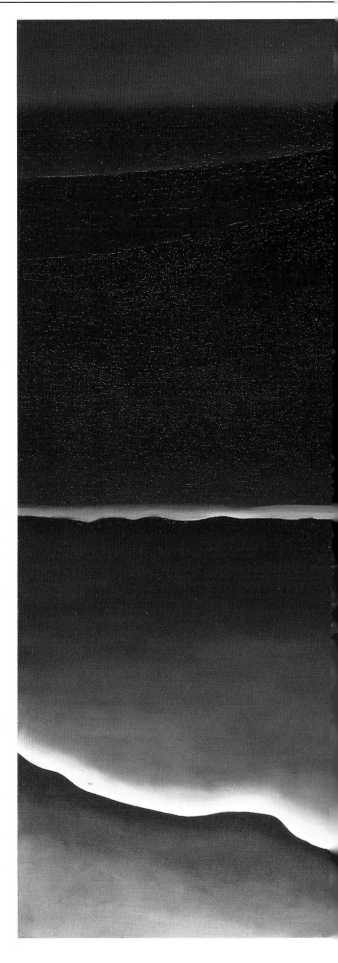

Georgia O'Keeffe made up her mind to be an artist when she was only ten years old. She trained at art college in Chicago and worked as a commercial artist and as a teacher of art. She continued to study painting until one day in 1915, when she was twenty-eight years old, she gathered all her work together and she looked at it carefully. She decided that she had learned nothing of value, so she destroyed it all and started again. O'Keeffe was determined to find her own way of painting and to peel off all the layers of teaching that prevented her from doing this.

O'Keeffe worked alone, making black and white drawings in charcoal. She sent them to a close friend in New York for her opinion but asked her not to show them to anyone else. The friend took them to a dealer who liked them very much and without telling the painter, exhibited the drawings. As it happened O'Keeffe was visiting New York and she went to the gallery to make the dealer take her drawings down. That was the first time she met the man who was to become her friend, her adviser and her husband.

Finding her style

In New York O'Keeffe met other painters and became part of the Precisionist group. The Precisionists tried to make very precise and accurate copies of the real world. But O'Keeffe's paintings were always different and showed a very personal style. She preferred to paint flowers, or bones, often exaggerating their size and setting them in rocky landscapes which have a feeling of vast empty space and clear light. Where the other Precisionists are often cold and clinical, O'Keeffe's work is elegant. Her subject matter is often extremely simple. This picture, *Wave, Night*, is simply of the surface of the water and the waves as they break on the beach. The water creeps up, changing from indigo to lilac. The foam edges the waves like embroidery on the edge of a cloth. Currents in the water lead our eyes towards a tiny light, the beam from a lighthouse, peeping over the horizon. The picture shows how it is possible to draw with colour instead of line.

Addison Gallery of American Art, Phillips Academy, Andover, Massachusetts

Fuji seen through the Waves off Kanagawa

Woodcut 24.6 × 36.5 cm

Katsushika Hokusai
LIVED:
1760-1849

NATIONALITY:
Japanese

TYPE OF WORK:
prints from woodcut blocks

Prints made from blocks cut out in wood were a very popular art form in Japan from the seventeenth to the nineteenth centuries. Hundreds of artists produced many thousands of these pictures. Popular printmakers such as Hokusai and Hiroshige (see pages 16 and 44) were in great demand. There was always pressure from their publishers to keep producing new work. As many as two hundred copies of each print would be made and often they were all sold on the day they were published. Hokusai is said to have made 30 000 drawings in his long career, and to have produced 500 books.

Learning throughout his life

Hokusai was a very humble man. He said that although he began to draw at the age of six, it was not until he was in his sixties that he understood how to draw animals and plants well. Another time he said that he could not draw until he was seventy years old, and that nothing he had done before that was satisfactory. This print is from a series called, *Thirty-six Views of Mount Fuji*, which Hokusai began when he was about sixty years old.

Balance and form

Hokusai was interested in decorative, abstract works rather than in realism. His landscapes have a wonderful sense of balance because he gave form and structure to the scenes he painted. His work is also, as in the case of this picture, strikingly dramatic. The great curling wave which lifts menacingly over the little boats is boldly drawn in black and white against the yellow sky. Mount Fuji itself is dwarfed by the wave which, with its tentacles of foam, has the appearance of a sea monster.

A team effort

The artist made his drawing on a sheet of thin paper which was then stuck down on to a piece of wood. Expert engravers cut the drawing lines into the wood and the picture was then printed in black only. The artist coloured the print by hand. More blocks were made, one for each of the colours to be used, and then each block was printed on top of the other. Great care has been taken to make sure that each printing matched exactly. Metallic dust and shiny mica could also be used to produce the effect the artist wanted.

Sunset over the Sea

Tapestry, from an original watercolour 242.5 ×180cm

John Houston

John Houston

BORN:
1930

NATIONALITY:
British

TYPE OF WORK:
landscape paintings

DIRECTOR OF WEAVING:
Fiona Matheson

The Dovecot Studio in Edinburgh revived the old tradition of tapestry weaving at the beginning of this century. Over the last thirty years there has been a growing interest in tapestry and many artists have designed work which will become a woven picture. The word tapestry comes from 'tapis', the French word for carpet, but these 'carpets' are not made to go on the floor. They follow an old tradition of hanging carpets on the wall, not just to look at but also to keep the draughts out.

A painter concerned with colour

John Houston is a Scottish landscape painter. His work was chosen by the Dovecot Studio when they wanted to draw attention to the work of Scottish artists. The original picture from which they worked was a watercolour, with brilliant, transparent areas of colour running into each other. A magnificent sunset colours the sky and the water completely. Even the lumpy black rocks have taken on the sunset's pinkish glow.

A problem for the weavers

The gradual blending of the colours in the picture posed a problem for the weavers. It was solved by the very careful mixing of coloured threads in the strands as they were being woven. One thread at a time was changed as the colour moved from yellow to red, so that the change was very subtle and gentle. You can probably see how some of it was done by looking closely. Sometimes the thread was made thicker so that there was more strength to a brilliant patch of colour. Sometimes the thread was changed from wool, which is strong and deep in its colour, to cotton, which has a more reflective quality.

Just as Houston chose from a range of colours, mixing paint to produce exactly the effect he wanted, so the weavers mix colour. First they mix dyes to get a range of coloured threads, and then they mix the threads to produce a range of colours.

This combination of the work of artist and craft worker is common in the production of works of art. The artist printmaker works with the craft printer, the sculptor in bronze cooperates with the foundry worker.

Summer Night

Oil on canvas 100.5 × 135.5 cm

Kitty Kielland

LIVED:
1843-1914

NATIONALITY:
Norwegian

TYPE OF WORK:
landscape paintings

Nasjonalgalleriet, Oslo

Kitty Kielland began to paint seriously at the age of thirty. She trained first in Norway and then in 1875 at the Art School for Women in Munich. Then with her Norwegian companion she arrived in Paris where she met painters from all over Europe. She always painted out of doors and is best known for landscapes with water which she always gave a mirror-clear consistency.

One summer Kielland and a group of Norwegian artists who had met in Paris returned to Norway to a farm on the shores of Lake Daelivannet. They spent the summer drawing and painting. This picture of the lake was one of the most successful of that summer.

The blue hour

In Norway the summer evenings are long and light. As the sun sets there is a time known as 'the blue hour'. In the dusk of the blue hour shapes are simplified, colour loses its intensity and everything is softened. In this light the water reflects the dark hillside and the pastel sky. A fringe of reeds stands sharply in the foreground, and water lily pads break the water's gleaming surface. A breeze ripples the water where the dark reflection meets the light. On the edge of the lake the water breaks and laps silvery on the black deep. A rowing boat is just visible pulling across the lake in the half-light.

A style to capture the atmosphere

Kielland's painting is full of the atmosphere of the strange 'blue hour'. It makes a remarkable contrast with Kokoschka's lake painting (page 25). Can you imagine being in each of these places? What would you be feeling if you visited them?

Nasjonalgalleriet, Oslo

Jinker on a Sandbank

Oil on canvas 152.3 × 122 cm

Arthur Boyd

BORN:
1920

NATIONALITY:
Australian

TYPE OF WORK:
paintings, ceramics, prints, drawings, stage design

Arthur Boyd was one of five children, all of whom became artists. The Boyd family was very artistic, Boyd's father was a potter, and his mother, one grandmother and both grandfathers were painters.

With so much art around him it is not surprising that Boyd started to paint early in his life. He learned mainly from his family, though after he left school he took evening classes at the Australian National Gallery Art School. He worked in his uncle's paint factory during the day. Boyd had his first solo exhibition at the age of seventeen.

Great variety

Boyd worked in many media. He made ceramic sculptures and ceramic paintings, paintings in oil and watercolour and, for a while, he painted on small copper plates. He made drawings in ink and pencil and pastels. His prints were etchings, lithographs and aquatints.

The subjects Boyd paints are as varied as the materials he works with. His family was deeply religious and throughout his work he chose to illustrate stories from the Bible. He has also found subjects in the Australian landscape and its mythology. Boyd has a real and deep understanding of the plight of the Aboriginal peoples and the destruction of their culture by the new world.

Boyd's techniques in painting vary, too. Sometimes he works with paint which he puts on in wide, wild-looking brush strokes. Sometimes he produces the controlled smoothness of the picture we see here, in which it is hard to find the mark of the brush. The setting sun is tinting the sky, the cliffs and the water with a delicate pink. The skyline has a strength and clarity against the paleness of the sky. The water is smooth as glass. Against this tranquillity is placed an oddly-shaped group of little black figures in silhouette. The birds appear to be menacing the horse as the driver of the jinker, a little cart, tugs at the reins. Boyd frequently mixed fantasy with reality, myth with observation. Perhaps that is what we see in this mysterious picture.

Fischer Fine Art

Lac d'Annecy II

Oil on canvas 75.5 × 100.6 cm

Oskar Kokoschka

LIVED:
1886-1980

NATIONALITY:
Born in Vienna, Austria, Kokoschka became a British citizen in 1947

TYPE OF WORK:
oil and watercolour paintings, book illustration

Museum of Modern Art, New York © COSMOPRESS, Geneva/DACS London 1988

Oscar Kokoschka was a wanderer. He was born in Vienna, but fled from Germany to England in 1938 when his work was condemned. He answered by painting a defiant picture and called it *Self Portrait of a Degenerate Artist*. He died aged ninety-four, in Switzerland. Between times he visited and painted in many countries.

This picture was painted during Kokoschka's travels in 1930. He painted landscapes and portraits and gave to both an extraordinary, expressive quality. His work is classed with that of the group of painters known as the German Expressionists. He used colour not to mimic reality but to express his feelings. His colours are vibrant and strong, and his brush was used speedily, leaving in a trail of paint the record of his movements. Kokoschka liked to find a place from which he looked down on his subject. He often painted two views of the same subject from opposite positions, so that his understanding of the place had an all-round quality. His pictures took at longest a fortnight but sometimes only a day or two to complete.

Translucent light

Water fascinated Kokoschka. He painted rivers and lakes and the sea beating against the shore. He caught the light on the water and at the same time he makes it look deep. He used oil paint thinned with turpentine to achieve a translucent effect.

In this painting, a brilliant sky, multi-coloured by the setting sun, is reflected in the deep blue mirror of the lake. Light catches on the waves like the facets of a sapphire. The hillside and the town across the lake are deep purple and green in the shadow. Little black boats are just visible on the water.

A celebration of life

The painting is a celebration. In the First World War Kokoschka fought at the battle front. He said long afterwards, 'And then I thought . . . if ever I come out of this rat-existence alive, I will paint landscapes, because I have seen so little of the world, so I want to see everywhere, I want to go everywhere . . .'

The Phillips Collection, Washington © COSMOPRESS, Geneva/DACS
London 1988

Fur Traders descending the Missouri

Oil on canvas 73.5 × 92.5 cm

George Caleb Bingham

LIVED:
1811-1879

NATIONALITY:
American

TYPE OF WORK:
portraits, landscapes

George Caleb Bingham grew up on the banks of the Mississippi River in Missouri in the southern part of the United States of America. He taught himself to draw and paint, and travelled around earning a living by painting portraits. In 1841 at the age of thirty he spent three months as a student at an art college in Philadelphia. He began to paint scenes from everyday life, and his paintings of river people attracted special attention.

This painting is of a fur trader, his son and their pet bear cub going down the river in their narrow dugout canoe. They are taking furs to New Orleans for sale. The painting was sold for 75 dollars to The American Art Union. The Union ran a lottery which enabled its members to receive an engraving of a painting each year and a chance to win the original work. This painting was won by a subscriber from Alabama.

Water in morning light

The river is seen in the morning light. The mists which rise from the water veil the shore. The water itself is calm and flat. The strange light which catches the edge of the trees, lights the traders dramatically from one side. It casts an orange glow on the water. The reflections are direct and have an odd, heavy quality. The light and the stillness give the water a solid and mirror-like substance and yet we see it quietly flowing by. The figures in the boat stand out strongly as they glide along but at the same time they have been very carefully placed. Their bodies, together with the clump of trees behind them, make a satisfying shape. They do not poke up above the level of the trees, their curved backs echo the tree shapes, and the boy's head joins one clump to the next.

The gentle calm of the early morning and the relaxation of the traders is caught by Bingham. The wide waters of the great river are in a peaceful mood.

The Metropolitan Museum of Art, New York, Morris K. Jessup Fund, 1933

Early Morning on the Seine

Oil on canvas 81.5 × 93 cm

Claude Monet

LIVED:
1840-1926

NATIONALITY:
French

TYPE OF WORK:
oil paintings, drawings

The Tate Gallery, London © DACS 1988

Claude Monet is probably the painter most people think of first when the Impressionists are mentioned. They were a group of artists who lived in and around Paris and worked quite closely together for several years, sharing their ideas and often travelling together to paint.

A new vision

Monet wanted to see the world about him without the clutter of old ideas. He wanted to see it naturally and with fresh eyes. He said that he would like to paint, '. . . as a bird sings . . .' On another occasion Monet said that he would like to have been born blind, then to gain his sight just as he was ready to start painting, so that he saw things for the first time without knowing what they were. From the style of painting that he chose and developed throughout his long career, we can begin to see what Monet meant. He became best known for his paintings of the natural world, but he also painted scenes from modern life.

More than one glance

Sometimes Monet painted a series of pictures about one subject. He certainly made two paintings of the view of the River Seine that we see in this picture. He painted both pictures in the early morning light, in the same year, on canvases of almost the same size, but the two works are not at all alike. The colour Monet used – the colours he *saw* – are entirely different. A different day, a different moment and Monet's keen eye saw what is almost a different place.

Half this painting is of water, filled with reflections. On this slightly misty morning it is hard to tell where dry land ends and reflection begins. Hundreds of tiny delicate brush strokes blend together in our mind's eye to create a moment of magic.

The Metropolitan Museum of Art, New York, Bequest of Julian W. Emmons, 1956
© DACS 1988

The Banks of the Seine near Vétheuil

Oil on canvas 73 × 100cm

Claude Monet

LIVED:
1840-1926

NATIONALITY:
French

TYPE OF WORK:
oil paintings, drawings

The Tate Gallery, London © DACS 1988

Monet lived near the River Seine for most of his life. He loved water and the plants and trees that grow around water. He painted the river many times throughout his life. In his home at Giverny Monet had a setion of river diverted to flow through his garden and there he created a lake with ornamental bridges and weeping willows, lilies and rushes. Then he set about painting the garden he had made.

A different touch

This painting was made nearly twenty years before *Early Morning on the Seine*. The way in which Monet uses the paint is quite different in the two pictures. In this work we are much more aware of the brush marks. Their direction and the thickness of the paint give form to the objects they depict. The water reflects the sky, but the quality of the surface of water and sky is quite different. Each area of the painting has a rhythm of marks, horizontal or vertical, light or heavy, which give the picture its richness. Look at the dark green lines of the stalks of the plants. It is possible to imagine Monet's hand moving across the canvas in a steady march as he made them. Then look at the light touches which are the daisy heads. Can you really see daisies or are you just imagining them?

Fading sight

At the end of his life Monet was troubled by fading sight. Cararacts on both eyes were diagnosed. An operation on one eye was partially successful, enabling Monet to work on his last great project. It was a painting, two metres high and 8.5 metres long, of water lilies in a vibrant pool of green and purple. Water and its plants occupied Monet's talents for nearly sixty years.

National Gallery of Art, Washington, Chester Dale Collection © DACS 1988

The Bridge at Courbevoie

Oil on canvas 64.5 × 82.3 cm

Georges Seurat

LIVED:
1859-1891

NATIONALITY:
French

TYPE OF WORK:
drawings and paintings

Philadelphia Institute of Art

Georges Seurat developed a style of painting known as *Pointillism*. He had a scientist's attitude towards painting, studying the theory of colour and of light. Seurat made his own paintings by putting very small dots of bright colour one on top of another instead of mixing them on a palette.

The careful worker

The paintings took Seurat hours and hours to do. He was a perfectionist in every way. He often painted a border around his paintings in a darker tone, but still using his pointillist method, so that shadows thrown by the picture frame would be hidden. Sometimes he painted the frame in pointillist dots as well!

Seurat first learned about colour from the Impressionist painters, but he went further than they did in his study and his experiments. Unlike the Impressionists, he rarely painted out-of-doors, but like them he made the same thorough studies of the subjects of his paintings.

Shimmering pictures

Seurat's style is demonstrated clearly in this picture of the River Seine. The water reflects the sky, the sailing boat and the line of poles. The little dots of paint make the surface of the water shimmer. Compare the way in which Seurat has painted the near shore and his treatment of the further shore. He makes the dots less obvious when the colours are paler in the distance and strongest in contrast in the bark of the leafless tree and in the autumn colours on the river bank. Compare this picture with Monet's of the Seine. Do you think they were equally successful in painting the water?

Courtauld Institute Galleries, London

The River

Oil on canvas 60 × 73 cm

Maurice de Vlaminck

LIVED:
1876-1958

NATIONALITY:
French

TYPE OF WORK:
paintings, woodcuts and
lithographic illustrations

Maurice de Vlaminck was not trained as a painter and he was proud of the fact. He boasted that he had never set foot in the Louvre, the great museum of art in Paris, and that the École des Beaux Arts, the main college for art in Paris, should be burnt down! Vlaminck believed that painters should work from instinct. If they did, their own ideas and feelings would be expressed in their work. He thought that each painter began at a fresh starting point in art and should not refer to the past. Nevertheless Vlaminck did work with other painters, learning a great deal from Van Gogh, then from Matisse and from Cézanne.

Attention to structure

The River is from the period when Vlaminck paid much attention to the form and structure of his paintings. The buildings in the picture have a very solid look and they are drawn in perspective. The two framing trees on either side give scale to the scene, and the diagonal line of the river and the horizontal skyline cut the canvas into an interesting patchwork. Vlaminck was influenced by the work of the painter Cézanne at the time.

The water in this picture has been painted in a different way from many others we have seen. It is seen entirely as a reflection. It has no ripples, no waves, no movement of its own. It is just an up-side-down and slightly distorted version of the land. And yet there is no doubt that it *is* water. It also has an incredible smoothness which is odd as the brush marks are rough and strong.

Strong colour

The colour scheme for the picture is strong too. The boldly contrasting warm reds and pinks of the houses seem to be bathed in sunlight against the shadowy greens of the woods. The sky, filled with billowing cloud, is tinged with purple against its greeny blue.

National Gallery of Art, Washington, Chester Dale Collection © DACS 1988

The Deep

Duco and oil on canvas 200.4 × 150.2 cm

Jackson Pollock

LIVED:
1912-1956

NATIONALITY:
American

TYPE OF WORK:
paintings

Jackson Pollock brought new ideas and methods to painting. He was an innovator. He experimented with ideas and he experimented with paint. In 1947 he made a bold move. Instead of putting his canvas on a frame on an easel he stretched it out on the floor. He abandoned his brushes and began to pour and drip ordinary household paint from tins on to the canvas. Then he moved the paint around with sticks trowels and knives. Pollock said that he felt closer to his paintings when they were on the floor. He could walk round them, work from all sides, or be literally in the middle of the painting if he chose. He sometimes added sand, bits of broken glass and other objects to give texture to his paintings. He had an intense awareness of surfaces and textures. This interest may have sprung from years he spent as a surveyor in California and Arizona where the pattern and colour of the rock formations are rich and varied.

Feelings and movement

Pollock's style became known as Action Painting for the obvious reason that it required a much more violent action than wielding a brush. He was also known as an Abstract Expressionist. He felt that his movement in painting gave expression to his feelings at the very moment that he painted. He agreed with the idea explored by Picasso that Art is the expression of our unconscious thought. He did not paint a picture of any object or place when he used this style. He was allowing something to come out of himself in the act of painting. At the same time that Pollock made his 'splash and dribble' paintings, he also made more conventional landscapes. For the last three years of his life he returned to using a brush and only occasionally dribbled the paint.

The rebel

Pollock had never been interested in tradition. He was a rebel in one way or another throughout his life. He was expelled from high school when he edited a paper which spoke out too strongly against authority. In his work he abandoned all the rules and did something completely new.

Musée d'Art Moderne, Paris © ARS 1988

Untitled

Paint on bark 103 × 59 cm

Johnny Mundrugmundrug

LIVED:
c.1925 to 1988

NATIONALITY:
Australian

TYPE OF WORK:
ceremonial dancing and singing,
painting

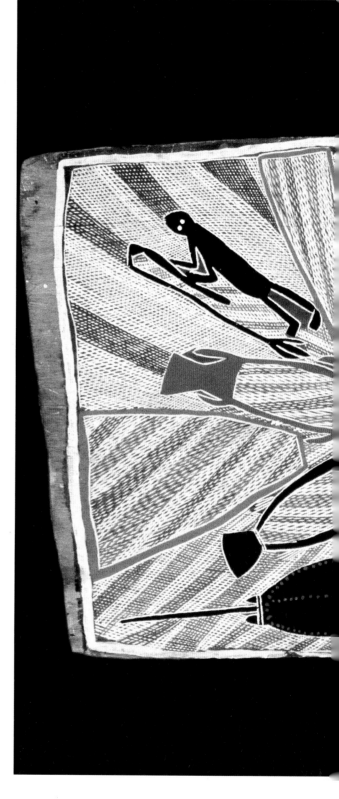

Australian Aboriginal bark paintings are an essential part of a performance art which includes dancing and especially singing. This painting and its songs are sung and danced by related people from a particular part of northern Australia.

The painting tells of the *wongar*, spirits who existed before human beings. These spirits were there in animals, objects and places. They are still all around. The Aborigines divide them into two groups, those which come from the land, and those from th sea and the coast. This painting shows creatures from the sea group. It also shows three 'Trickster' *wongar* which have taken on human shape.

The fine lines all over the picture show who is allowed to sing and paint the story. This area of hatching is also the water, because the fish swim in it and are speared by the Tricksters. The fishes' home is the white circle in the centre of the painting. Like stained glass windows in churches, bark paintings not only give pleasure, they remind people of a sacred story and its meanings. Mundrugmundrug's style is unmistakably Aboriginal and has meanings which are known only to members of his group.

The materials

Aboriginal artists have been painting their stories for 40 000 years. They painted first on rocks but concentrate now on bark paintings. Their ancestors used coloured clays and brushes made from plants and twigs. Today the artists also use commercial paints and brushes. Whatever the materials, the importance of their art work continues.

An offer of friendship

This painting is part of a set made for a *Rom* ceremony which took place in Canberra in 1982. The aim of *Rom* ceremonies is to celebrate friendship between groups. The Canberra *Rom* ceremony was extraordinary because it cemented friendship with non-Aboriginal peoples. Mundrugmundrug was an important figure at this ceremony, also taking part in the dancing and singing.

Mundrugmundrug died in 1988. There is no portrait of him in this book because Aboriginal peoples do not allow the use of photographs of anyone who has recently died.

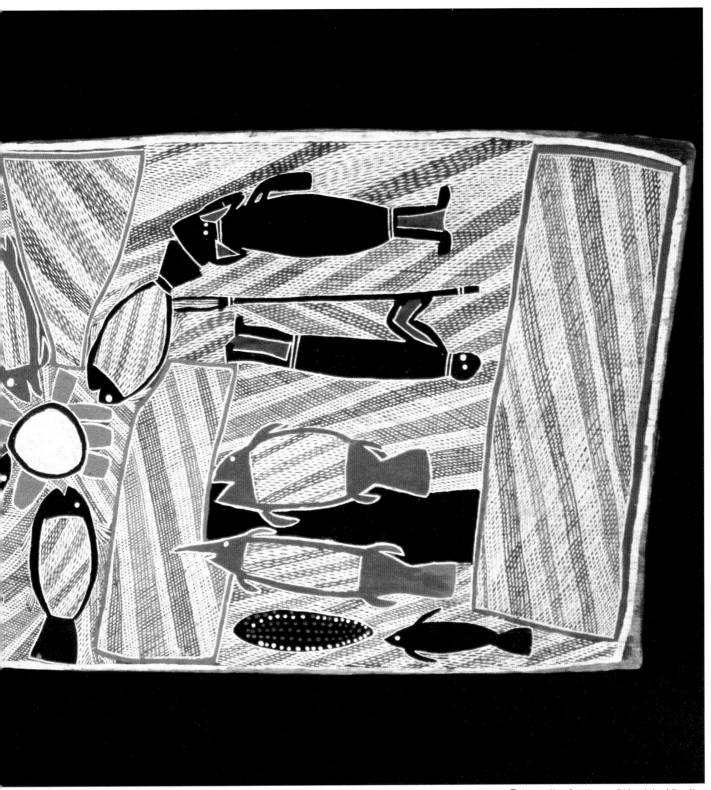

A Diver (Paper Pool No. 17)

Coloured paper pulp 183 × 434 cm

David Hockney

BORN:
1937

NATIONALITY:
British

TYPE OF WORK:
paintings, prints stage design, photography

David Hockney has been a successful painter from the time he left the Royal College of Art in 1962. He won four major prizes in his last year at college and two years later he held his first solo exhibition.

In 1963 Hockney went to live in California and it was there that he started to paint swimming pools. He returned to Europe and lived in Paris where he learnt the techniques of etching. Hockney becomes almost obsessed with a new technique, exploring it thoroughly. In 1978 he went back to America intending to paint again but discovered the paper pulp technique at a friend's studio outside New York City.

Back to pools

Hockney chose to go back to his old interest in swimming pools for this new medium. He worked for three months, taking only one day off, and made twenty-nine pictures, all based on the swimming pool at the studio. He used a polaroid camera to take photographs of the pool at various times of the day with different lights and shadows on it. Sometimes he made pictures of the pool at night, sometimes in bright daylight. Sometimes the pool was empty and sometimes, as in this case, the water contained a shadowy swimming figure.

The technique

To make the pictures, sheets of pulped rag, the substance from which paper is made, were laid out freshly made and still wet. Hockney poured coloured dye on to the wet pulp, controlling it by using frames to contain certain colours. Then the whole sheet was put through a press and the paper pulp squashed into a sheet. Sometimes Hockney would half press the work and then add more colour. The green squiggles on the surface of the water are done in this way. When dry, the colour was deeply embedded in the paper and had a greater intensity than if it were painted on the surface.

Hockney sat watching the water and the diver for hours at a time and he also drew. He worked out the patterns and found how to catch the movement by drawing in black and white first. Often at the end of the day he threw the work away because it did not match the idea in his head.

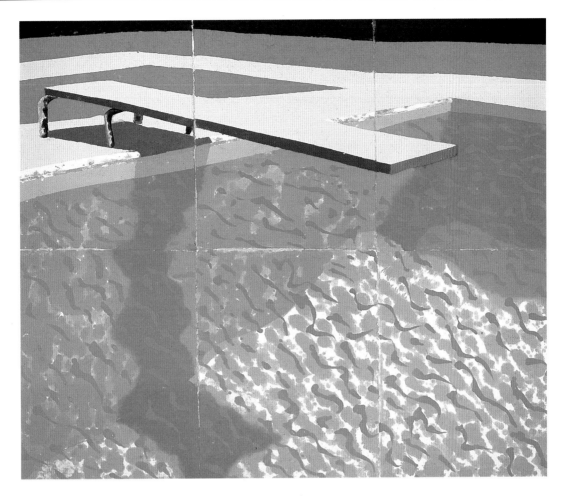

Leaping Cataract, Victoria Falls

Aquatint 20.2 × 12 cm

Patrick Procktor

Photograph Duncan Baxter

BORN:
1936

NATIONALITY:
Irish, came to England aged four

TYPE OF WORK:
prints, watercolours, oil paintings

Procktor was born in Ireland, but was brought to England by his widowed mother when he was a small child. He was a clever boy and wanted to study Latin and Greek at university, but his mother could not afford to keep him at school. He went to work for a builder's merchant when he was sixteen years old. During military service Procktor learned Russian and later he earned his living as a translator. All this time he had been painting whenever he could, and in 1958 he enrolled as a student at the Slade School of Fine Art in London. There he studied painting and printmaking. His prints were first published in 1968. By then he was well known as a painter first of in oils and then in watercolours. In was painting with watercolour that led Procktor towards the gentle tones that could be produced by means of aquatint.

Procktor's time in the army gave him a taste for travelling. He now spends much of his life abroad, making paintings wherever he goes. This picture is one of a series he made on a visit to South Africa. Procktor said about it, 'I wanted to get the intensity and translucency of the rainbow'.

The technique

The drawings were made on to two copper plates which were covered in resin. The lines of the drawings were cut into the plates using acid. Then ink was brushed over the plates and the pictures were printed on to paper. This process was repeated six times using different coloured inks. Each print is placed exactly on top of the next. Can you see where each colour has been printed? For this picture Procktor used greens, purple, blue, black and brown. If you have ever tried to take a print from ink or paint which has been spread out on a smooth surface, you can probably guess how Procktor achieved the effect of the rocks in the brown ink.

Downpour at Shono

Woodcut

Ando Hiroshige

LIVED:
1797-1858

NATIONALITY:
Japanese

TYPE OF WORK:
prints from woodcut blocks

Hiroshige was a very popular artist of *Ukiyo-e* or 'the floating world'. This is the name given to pictures produced by Japanese artists in the seventeenth to the nineteenth centuries. They painted objects and scenes from the fashionable but changing world around them. Landscapes were very popular. This picture is one of a series called, *Fifty-three Posting Stations of the Tokaido.* The series of fifty-five prints depicts scenes from a long journey on the road linking the towns of Edo and Kyoto, as it comes down through the mountains to the coast. The posting stations were places where weary travellers could rest. Hiroshige was a great traveller himself, and journeyed from end to end of the Japanese islands taking his sketchbooks with him and making notes on his way. His finished works were often imaginary, though based on his observations.

A master of atmosphere

Downpour at Shono is a very good example of Hiroshige's work. He was particularly good at creating an atmosphere. Sudden downpours, snow storms, overpowering heat were all subjects he could capture in his prints. He could also capture moments of sudden movement as we can see here in the helter-skelter of the people running for cover or trying to put up an umbrella. In Hiroshige's prints the people are an important part of the composition, equal to the natural aspects in the picture. Compare the people here with the people in the print by his rival, Hokusai, on page 17.

Subtle use of colour

Hiroshige has described the rain by the colours he has chosen, as well as in the drawing itself. The rain is so heavy that it falls like a net curtain, draining the colour from the trees and the houses. It is only around the poor travellers that it is possible to see colour through the deluge. The rain falls from a black and smoky sky and it looks as if there is more rain still to come.

Hiraki Ukiyo-e Foundation. Riccar Art Museum, Tokyo

Landscape in the Rain

Oil on canvas 50 × 100 cm

Vincent Van Gogh

	LIVED: 1853-1890
	NATIONALITY: Dutch
	TYPE OF WORK: drawings, oil paintings

The Metropolitan Museum of Art.

A painting by Vincent Van Gogh was sold at auction in November 1987 for £30 187 623. The sale highlights the tragedy of the man who painted it. He sold hardly any of his paintings during his lifetime. His work was much admired by fellow painters but did not appeal to the critics or to the public. He spent months at a time in an asylum, suffering from attacks of very serious mental illness. At the age of thirty-seven he shot himself in the chest and died two days later. This painting was among Van Gogh's last works.

A passion for painting

Van Gogh worked hard and fast, often completing a painting in a day. He painted for only ten years, but he made about 800 paintings and 800 drawings. He used his paint in a way which makes his work quite unique. He laid it on to his canvas thickly, in bold swirling strokes or short sudden stabs. Van Gogh was entranced by colour, but he used it to express feelings rather than painting the colours he saw exactly. He worked for many months in the south of France in bright light and a golden summer landscape. His most famous paintings are filled with the yellow that he loved. The inside of his room, his chair, and the jars full of sunflowers are filled with wonderful sunshine.

Typical Van Gogh

This picture is easily recognised as a Van Gogh because of the brushmarks and because of the colour. We see the roof tops of a village, hidden in a fold in the hill. Cypress trees, another favourite of Van Gogh's, poke their curly tops into the air. The fields are golden, perhaps it is the stubble of corn glistening in the rain, perhaps it is pasture parched by the summer sun. The whole scene is soaked in a sudden downpour of rain. The trees and the roof fall almost straight down, using a sharp edge to drag the colour down the canvas in streaks. It does not look as if the rain will last long though. The sky is lightening over the hill.

Although Van Gogh painted seriously for only a few years, he had been observing and drawing nature since childhood. He made endless studies of birds and plants and people. He also painted many portraits, of himself and of the people who befriended him.

BEDFORDSHIRE LEISURE SERVICES COUNTY COUNCIL

National Museum of Wales, Cardiff

Some ideas

For lovers of water

You may have read this book because you like water. If so perhaps you might try drawing streams or ponds or the sea near your home. Remember Hockney and his photographs and drawings? Looking with a painter's eyes could help you find out much more about what water is like.

For picture lovers

You may have read this book because you like looking at pictures. If so perhaps you would like to see the original works. Remember how Vlaminck learned from the work of other painters of his time and Turner learned from Claude? A list at the front of the book tells you where to find those paintings which are on view to the public. The paintings in this book are in collections all over the world so you will not be able to see them all. Your nearest gallery may have other works by the artists you like.

For those who want to have a go themselves

You may have read this book because you like to draw or paint. If so perhaps the book has helped you to discover some of the secrets of picture making. All the work that is in the book is the result of hard thinking, lots of practice and above all very careful looking. Remember how Hokusai learned through drawing all his life? Perhaps you could start a notebook now of landscape or seascape around you. You will soon collect the information that will help you to make your own ideas come alive.